William Wallace
Braveheart

PITKIN GUIDES

Map of Scotland, showing key sites

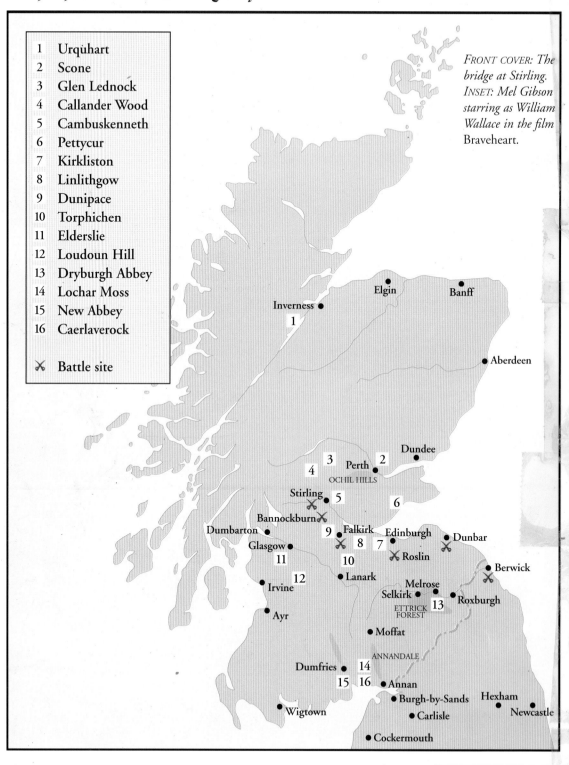

1 Urquhart
2 Scone
3 Glen Lednock
4 Callander Wood
5 Cambuskenneth
6 Pettycur
7 Kirkliston
8 Linlithgow
9 Dunipace
10 Torphichen
11 Elderslie
12 Loudoun Hill
13 Dryburgh Abbey
14 Lochar Moss
15 New Abbey
16 Caerlaverock

✂ Battle site

FRONT COVER: The bridge at Stirling. INSET: Mel Gibson starring as William Wallace in the film Braveheart.

Elgin
Banff
Inverness
1
Aberdeen

Dundee
3 Perth 2
4
OCHIL HILLS
Stirling 5
6
Bannockburn
Dumbarton 9 Falkirk Edinburgh Dunbar
Glasgow 8 7
11 10 Roslin
Lanark Berwick
12 Melrose
Irvine Selkirk 13 Roxburgh
ETTRICK
FOREST
Ayr
Moffat
ANNANDALE
Dumfries 14
15 16 Annan
Burgh-by-Sands Hexham
Wigtown Carlisle Newcastle
Cockermouth

William Wallace – Braveheart

This is the story of a landless second son of an obscure Scottish knight who, when barely out of his teens and living as an outlaw, raised an army of common people and drove the occupying English army out of Scotland. It was an age when men owed allegiance to their feudal lords who were constantly fighting among themselves. William Wallace gave the people a sense of national, rather than feudal, loyalty and lit the torch of Scottish independence. For almost a year he was the Guardian of Scotland, but the nobles had no taste for the low-born Wallace; they betrayed him to Edward I, the Hammer of the Scots, to save their own skins and estates. But Wallace continued a guerilla war against the English for six more years before finally being betrayed by one of his compatriots and taken to London, there to be executed as a traitor to a crown that he had never acknowledged. He did not die in vain; Bruce carried on his cause at Bannockburn.

ABOVE: William Wallace, by David Scott (1806–1849).

Important Dates

*c.*1272   William Wallace is born, probably at Elderslie, near Paisley.

1286   The Scottish king Alexander III dies.

1291   Edward I of England summons English and Scottish barons to Berwick. Scotland's independence is surrendered, and Scotland occupied by the English. Around this time, Wallace's first recorded affray with an Englishman takes place in Dundee.

1292   On Edward's instructions, John Balliol is crowned at Scone.

1293   At the English parliament, Balliol is found guilty of contempt of court, and the jurisdiction of Scotland is forfeited to Edward.

1296   Edward sacks Berwick and defeats Balliol at Dunbar. The Stone of Destiny is taken to Westminster. Balliol resigns the throne. John de Warenne, Earl of Surrey, is appointed Guardian of Scotland. Near this time, Wallace avenges his father's death at Loudoun Hill, near Lanark, and is declared an outlaw.

1297   Wallace kills Hazelrig, the Sheriff of Lanark, raises an army and defeats the English at the Battle of Stirling Bridge. He later leads an invasion of England.

1298   Wallace is appointed Guardian of Scotland. Edward defeats Wallace at the Battle of Falkirk. Wallace resigns. Robert Bruce and John Comyn (the Red) become joint Guardians of Scotland.

1303   Bruce and Comyn attack and rout an English army at Roslin, near Edinburgh.

1305   Wallace is betrayed by Sir John de Menteith, captured, taken to London, and executed.

Neighbours in Conflict

The year 1286 was a fateful one for the Scots when their king, Alexander III, a descendant of William the Lion, unexpectedly died. On a stormy night when riding to his new bride, Joleta, he became separated from his companions and plunged over the cliffs of Pettycur near Kinghorn. The children of his previous marriage to Margaret of England having predeceased him, he had two years earlier named his granddaughter Margaret (the 'Maid of Norway') – who lived in Norway with her father King Erik – to be his successor.

Under Alexander's rule the Scots had enjoyed 20 years of peace at home and abroad with a buoyant export trade. That peace was soon to be rudely broken. Six Guardians of the Peace were appointed as regents to govern Scotland, none of them judged to be serious contenders for the throne, of which there were several among the warlike Scottish chiefs. However, the *status quo* was held by a treaty between the magnates of Scotland and King Edward I of England for Margaret to marry Edward's five-year-old son, Lord Edward, so that the two dynasties would be joined, but with a binding understanding that Scotland would remain an independent state. Thus would peace and prosperity be maintained and Edward's ambition to unite the two countries be satisfied.

It was not to be. The child queen was taken ill on the voyage from Norway and died in Orkney, a sad event which was to bring Scotland generations of misery, bloodshed and poverty. A fierce controversy ensued about who should succeed to the throne. The line of William the Lion became extinct with the death of Margaret, so the descendants of his brother David, who had died in 1219, were the nearest heirs, giving John Balliol and Robert Bruce (grandfather of the future king) the strongest claims among no less than 14 contestants. Within months Bruce had seized the royal castles of Dumfries and Wigton as well as Balliol's castle at Buittle. It was a dangerous situation which threatened civil war.

ABOVE: Edward I with monks and bishops. Despite his ruthlessness, Edward was always very careful to behave correctly in matters of the Church and was in the habit of praying at holy shrines before battle.

LEFT: John Balliol (1240–1314/15) and his wife.

In the hope that he would act as a fair mediator, the Scottish nobles invited Edward to adjudicate. He immediately accepted and called the barons of the north of England and of Scotland to a meeting at Berwick in May 1291. There they were peremptorily informed that before any discussion began he must be recognised as Lord Paramount of Scotland and fealty be sworn to him by all, from earl to burgess, under pain of eviction. At the same time he ordered the sheriffs of York, Northumberland, Lancaster, Cumberland and Westmorland to send their feudal forces to Berwick.

To their eternal shame the Scottish chiefs caved in, led by Robert Bruce and John Balliol. There was little opposition, and the independence of Scotland was surrendered for the selfish interests of its nobles, who were afraid of losing not only their Scottish estates but also their English estates for which they owed allegiance to Edward. Having bent the great magnates to his will, Edward ordered the surrender of all Scottish castles into his hands to be held until after the succession, which was to be delayed for many months while Scotland suffered the indignity of occupation by the English.

RIGHT: Edward I invests his son Edward as Prince of Wales. Had Margaret, the Maid of Norway, survived to marry young Edward as planned, the history of Scotland might have been very different.

The Scottish Wars of Independence

With Scotland firmly at his feet, Edward resumed his role of umpire for the succession to the Scottish crown, and in the great hall of Berwick Castle on 17 November 1292 he declared: 'Bruce shall take nothing in the competition with Balliol, and John Balliol shall have seisin [possession] of this kingdom of Scotland.' But he was careful to add: 'This judgement shall not impair my claim on the property of Scotland'. So Balliol, a tractable vassal, was crowned at Scone on St Andrew's Day. Although the most important castles were then nominally

BELOW: In the sack of Berwick in 1296, the castle was saved by its substantial fortifications, which were superseded by the English bastions built in the 1570s.

surrendered to him, they were still occupied by their Anglo-Norman governors and garrisons.

Edward lost no time in humiliating Balliol, compelling him to appear in English courts as a defendant in various cases brought by his own subjects. Appearing at an English parliament in 1293 to answer an appeal about lands in Fife, Balliol lost his patience, whereupon he was judged guilty of contempt of court and the three principal towns and castles of Scotland with their royal jurisdiction were forfeited to Edward. With the country at the mercy of Edward's men, there were frequent skirmishes between English soldiery and bands of Scots. In one of these, a Scottish knight, Sir Malcolm Wallace, was killed by an English knight named Fenwick. An epic poem, written by Blind Harry in the 15th century but based on a contemporaneous document sent to Pope Boniface, tells of the Scot fighting on his knees after his sinews had been severed. Malcolm Wallace's violent death was to imbue his son, William, with a hatred of the English.

In desperation, Balliol appealed for help from the French, but in 1295 Edward, being well aware of the conspiracy and the active resistance of

the Scots, decided to teach them all a lesson they would never forget. With a force of 5,000 cavalry and 30,000 infantry, on 30 March 1296 he marched to sack Berwick, then the richest city in Scotland but virtually undefended. Some 17,000 men, women and children – almost the total population – were butchered. When Flemish merchants in a building called the Red House tried to defend it on behalf of their hosts, the building was fired and all 30 people inside burnt to death. Only the well-defended castle was spared, whereupon the commander, Sir William Douglas, promptly obtained terms from Edward. The sack of Berwick was a calculated act of terrorism by Edward to subdue the Scots.

Balliol sent a prelate to Edward to deliver his renunciation of his allegiance and fealty and then took up arms. A battle ensued at Dunbar on 27 April 1296 where 10,000 Scots perished, many Scottish nobles fleeing the field when the battle went against them. It was then that the coronation stone of Scotland, the Stone of Destiny, was taken from Scone to Westminster. In July 1297, Balliol resigned his throne; his humiliation was compounded by Edward ripping the royal insignia from his tabard. For three years he lived a reasonably comfortable life, despite some of it being spent in the Tower of London, before being sent into exile in France, never to return.

HARY

QVHAM THQWIS
THQW SCOT

Wallace the Guerilla

William Wallace was the son of Sir Malcolm Wallace, the laird of Elderslie, which is now a district of Paisley. At one time in his youth he lived with his uncle who was a cleric at Cambuskenneth Abbey outside Stirling. He grew up to be a fine, strong lad over 6ft (2m) tall, a giant among men of those times. As a second son with no land of his own, he was possibly rather wild, with a fiery temper which he was later to vent on the English. It was in Dundee that the first recorded affray took place between Wallace and Selby, the son of the English constable of Dundee castle. It is quite likely that this event took place in December 1291. Furious at his taunts, Wallace stuck his dirk into Selby's heart and escaped into the crowd of onlookers.

There were to be other tales of his becoming embroiled with Englishmen, and single-handedly despatching several at a time. His reputation as an anti-English firebrand attracted a small band of like-minded men with whom he lived a will-o'-the-wisp life in the south west of the country. Eventually at Loudoun Hill in the Irvine valley he ambushed Fenwick, the knight who had killed his father. It is said that although Wallace had

only 50 men against 200 soldiers, Fenwick was killed and the English scattered, leaving 100 dead together with a large amount of useful armour, weapons and horses. Wallace was subsequently declared an outlaw; this is thought to have happened around the time of Balliol's humiliating defeat by Edward in 1296.

After Loudoun, Wallace and his compatriots retreated into Ettrick Forest, a large impenetrable area without roads in which no army would dare move nor cavalry scouts enter. On its periphery were the towns of Selkirk, Moffat and Lanark, and it was in the latter that Wallace secretly courted Marion Braidfute, a beautiful young heiress. They may have been married in St Kentigern's, the now ruined parish church, but there is no

ABOVE: The ruins of St Kentigern's Church, Lanark, the old parish church where Wallace is thought to have married Marion.

RIGHT: A statue of Wallace on the outer wall of St Nicholas Church, Lanark, a town frequented by Wallace during his early years as an outlaw.

proof of that, nor that she bore him a daughter. What is known is that the Sheriff of Lanark, Hazelrig, had had her brother put to death. To avenge him, Wallace stole into town with some comrades and, after killing about 50 English soldiers, hid in Marion's house before fleeing back to the safety of the forest. Hazelrig, having failed to capture Wallace, executed Marion instead 'to deny Wallace of the woman he truly loved'. It was probably the biggest mistake any sheriff made. Wallace gathered a larger force and again crept into the town under darkness, overpowered the castle guards and killed Hazelrig in his bed, then struck down his son and 240 English soldiers, merchants and commoners, sparing only their women and priests.

News of the slaughter lit the fire of independence among the people and thousands joined Wallace's crusade. In a bold attack they took Scone and overran the neighbouring country.

With Wallace currently in the ascendancy, he was joined by several nobles including the young Robert Bruce who was destined to take up Wallace's cause after his death and eventually restore the Scottish crown. Soon most of the country was in revolt, and Edward ordered Sir Henry de Percy and Sir Robert de Clifford to restore order. They raised an army in the north and marched into Scotland via Annandale and Nithsdale to confront the Scots at Irvine. At this point the Scottish nobles decided that because Wallace was a plebeian they could no longer serve with him, and all but Sir Andrew Moray of Bothwell promptly surrendered to the English commanders. Not so the common people. They literally rampaged across Scotland, bewildering the English with their guerilla tactics and taking every castle in their path until they confronted the main English army outside Stirling.

ABOVE: Cambuskenneth Abbey near Stirling, where Wallace lived as a youth with his uncle, who was a cleric there.

The Battle of Stirling Bridge 1297

With his army swollen to 40,000 lightly armed foot soldiers and about 180 horses, Wallace took up position on the steep-sided high ground now known as Abbey Craig, looking across the Forth to Stirling and its vital castle. His men, who would have made most of their own weapons, used 12ft (4m) long spears, axes and knives and wore rough hide tunics or homespun cloth; few would have had helmets or any form of body armour.

The English Governor of Scotland, John de Warenne, Earl of Surrey, commanded a force of mail-clad cavalry, skilled longbowmen from Wales (the deadly longbows were at that time warfare's newest secret weapon) and well-weaponed infantry, in all numbering 60,000, with 8,000 in reserve. This was to be Wallace's first experience of a standing battle as against guerilla and harrying actions. If Warenne, with his stronger and more disciplined force, could engage Wallace's men he would achieve a decisive victory, and by killing or capturing Wallace end all opposition to Edward. But he had a problem. The Forth lay between him and his objective, and there was just one narrow wooden bridge across it. He rejected the suggestion of using a ford further upstream, which would have caught the enemy in the rear, on the grounds that it would divide his army; it is more likely that he suspected treachery. While he hesitated, Hugh de Cressingham, Edward's Treasurer of Scotland, protested against 'the waste of the king's money, in keeping up an army, if it was not to fight'.

With that prod and the encouragement of his men, many of them seasoned veterans of Flanders and

Wales, Warenne ordered that the infantry should start crossing the bridge at dawn the following day, 11 September 1297. The flat ground beyond the bridge was marshy, and any attack would have to be made along a causeway and then uphill. From Abbey Craig, Wallace had a perfect view of the thin file of English fanning out from the bridge to pick their way hesitantly over the treacherous ground while his force lay in hiding at the foot of the Ochil Hills on their flank. It was the perfect situation for an ambush, with Wallace able to dictate the terms on which he would fight.

At the critical moment he gave the order and the Scots charged down the slopes to reach the bridgehead and trap a manageable number of the enemy who perished in their thousands, caught between Scottish spears and the river. What cavalry had crossed the bridge was soon floundering in the boggy ground, and those fighting to get back over it were blocked by those still advancing. Only

one, Sir Marmaduke de Twenge, succeeded; he spurred his horse through the press at the bridge, no doubt killing and injuring many of them. His reward from Warenne was the order to assemble whatever forces he could muster and occupy the now doomed Stirling Castle. Warenne himself then mounted his horse and rode for the safety of Berwick. Cressingham, who had an odious reputation even among the English and had been particularly barbaric in oppressing the Scots, was killed in the battle.

The Scottish losses at Stirling Bridge were relatively light, but the great loss to Wallace was the death of his faithful friend and joint general Sir Andrew Moray. This victory, followed by a string of successes, including the surrender of Edinburgh Castle, quickly restored Wallace to the favour of the vacillating Scottish nobles. Campaigning in Flanders, Edward received the news that 'this leader of a little band of outlaws, this plebeian without family, influence or wealth, supported by merit alone, had wrenched from the English every fortress in Scotland' (save Berwick).

LEFT: The old bridge across the Forth outside Stirling is thought to stand very near to the site of the original wooden bridge, where the battle was fought.

OPPOSITE: Wallace Memorial on Abbey Craig, Stirling, showing the position between Abbey Craig, where Wallace commanded the battle, and the Ochil Hills from where his men swept down onto the bridge.

BELOW: The Battle of Stirling Bridge.

Wallace Invades England

After clearing the English out of Scotland, Wallace turned his mind for a time to the administration of the country, and one of his early intentions was to resume commercial and diplomatic ties with Europe and win back the overseas trade which Scotland had enjoyed under Alexander III. Any evidence of his administrative acumen was probably destroyed by Edward's officials after his execution. There is, however, one Latin document in the archives of the Hanseatic town of Lubeck, signed by Wallace in October 1297, which told Lubeck and Hamburg that their merchants now had free access to all parts of the kingdom of Scotland, which had, by favour of God, been recovered by war from the power of the English.

Only one week after this document was signed, Wallace picked up the sword to mount an invasion of England. Crossing into Northumberland, the Scots followed the English army fleeing south in disarray. Caught between two armies, hundreds of refugees fled to safety behind the walls of Newcastle. The Scots laid waste a swathe of the countryside before wheeling west into Cumberland and pillaging all the way to Cockermouth. Then, hearing that the refugees in Northumberland were returning to their homes, Wallace led his men back east and fired 700 villages. There was a story, found in a letter written to the king of France, that Wallace's men rounded up 200 schoolchildren in Hexham, locked them in the old grammar school and incinerated them, but this is likely to have been just propaganda. What is true is that he gave the Prior of Hexham a letter of protection; but his followers nevertheless stole the chalice, altar ornaments and missal during Mass, whereupon Wallace had to admit to the canons that he had no control over his men.

Wallace's expedition into England brought the Scots great booty as well

LEFT: Carlisle Castle. The great border stronghold of the English, first built by William I, was frequently besieged by the Scots, including Wallace, without success. It was a major depot for supplies for Edward I's forces.

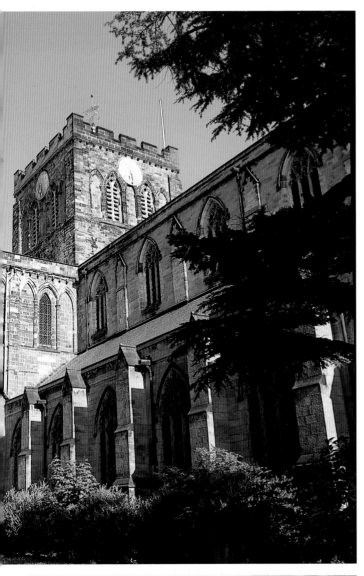

LEFT: Hexham Abbey, Northumberland, where Wallace's men ran riot.

as satisfying their appetites for slaughtering English. Without siege engines, Wallace was unable to make any impression on the English strongholds in the north – in fact he was careful to avoid them – and when the Newcastle garrison marched out to battle with him in November he wisely turned north and ran for home. There was another Scottish army in the west, known as the Men of Galloway, who were still besieging Carlisle Castle, but by December they had run out of provisions and retreated back across the Solway. Sir Robert de Clifford, Warden of the Western Marches, mounted a revenge raid into Scotland with his troops from the castle and local levies. Several towns and villages were burned, and over 300 Scots massacred at Lochar Moss. After a Christmas rest, de Clifford resumed the attack and in February destroyed Annan. This small but vicious little local war was mounted largely in retaliation against young Robert Bruce, Earl of Carrick, who was suspected of having taken up arms against the English, although he took no part in the Battle of Stirling Bridge or its subsequent events.

On his return from England, loaded with booty, Wallace found himself at the pinnacle of his power.

LEFT: Wallace Tower, Ayr. On 18 June 1297 the local leading Scots were summoned in the name of Edward I to the Barns of Ayr (barracks). As each man entered, he was swiftly strung up to die. In all, 360 were executed. In revenge, Wallace torched all the houses of the English.

Guardian of Scotland

By March 1298, Wallace had been knighted, reputedly by one of the leading earls of Scotland, and been appointed Guardian of Scotland. As such he became *de facto* King of Scotland but, seemingly harbouring no personal ambition, he declared that he had fought and now ruled in the name of John Balliol, his king in exile. He was to rule for less than a year. Although the Scottish nobles appeared to have accepted Wallace's leadership after the

RIGHT: Wallace made Guardian of Scotland. A statue by the Earl of Buchan.

Battle of Stirling Bridge and his English expedition, he had little faith in their support and set about dismantling the system of feudal vassalage and replacing it with a proper militia which would owe allegiance to Scotland rather than to individual chiefs. He planned to divide the country into military areas in which rolls would be maintained of all men between 16 and 60 capable of carrying arms. It was a form of conscription, and he was not squeamish about threatening draft-dodgers with the gibbet. He did not achieve much, however, in the way of administration in the very short time

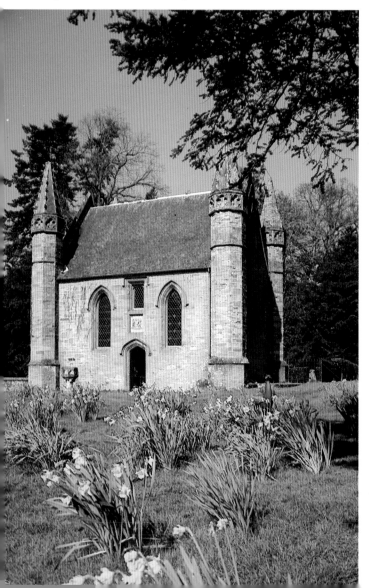

LEFT: The chapel on Moot Hill (also known as Boot Hill) at Scone. This is the site of early Scottish parliaments and the place where, in 1298, Wallace routed Edward I's justiciar, William de Ormsby, while the latter was holding court there.

before war intervened again.

Preparations for a new English expedition against the Scots had been put in hand after the defeat at the Battle of Stirling Bridge, although Edward himself was bogged down with a war in Flanders. In October 1297, orders were given to raise 35,000 levies and for provisions to be shipped from east coast ports to Newcastle. Further levies were to be raised in Wales and marched to Durham and Newcastle. All was to be ready by 28 January 1298. On 14 January, a parliament was held at York to which the Scottish magnates had been summoned in Edward's name. It is remarkable evidence of Wallace's standing at that time that not one of the Scottish nobles answered the summons to York.

Warenne, defeated at Stirling, was nevertheless again appointed to command the English army. Marching north from Newcastle, he quickly relieved Roxburgh and Berwick while the Scots fell back before his overwhelming forces, contenting themselves as before with guerilla-style attacks. A despatch from Edward announcing a peace treaty with France and ordering Warenne to stay at Berwick pending his own arrival brought a pause in the fighting, during which Wallace initiated a scorched-earth policy to deny the enemy any chance of living off the land as they advanced. Provisions were shipped from Ireland to Carlisle, and supply ships were made ready to sail to Berwick and Edinburgh when the latter fell into English hands.

Edward arrived at Roxburgh in June to find his army ready to march. This time the English mustered 3,000 armoured cavalry, 4,000 unarmoured horses and 8,000 mainly Irish and Welsh foot soldiers, the latter with their longbows. Edward reached Kirkliston without sighting the Scots, and there he had to wait anxiously for his provision ships which were stormbound. Because the countryside had been cleared by Wallace, the army was close to starvation. The Scots remained hidden, waiting for a chance to harass the English when hunger forced them to retreat. With increasing upset in the camp and hunger gnawing at his men, Edward gave the order to prepare to retreat to Edinburgh. It must have been the bitterest decision of his life. But at the last moment Wallace was once again betrayed; Edward consequently reversed his order and told the army to prepare for battle.

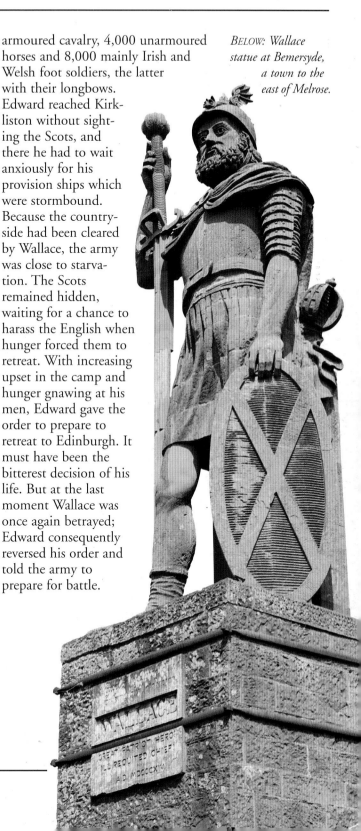

BELOW: Wallace statue at Bemersyde, a town to the east of Melrose.

The Battle of Falkirk

As the famished English army prepared to limp back to Edinburgh, the Earls of Angus and Dunbar (both in the army of Edward I) came to the English camp to tell them that Wallace and his army were hiding 15 miles away in Callander Wood, south of Falkirk, waiting to harass the English when they retreated. On hearing this very welcome news, Edward cried out: 'Thanks be to God, who hitherto hath delivered me from every danger; they need not chase after me, I will go forth and meet them.' That night the English lay in the fields east of Linlithgow with their arms beside them, each horse beside its rider. They were not only hungry but jittery. An alarm went up that the Scots were attacking, and in the panic Edward's horse kicked him, breaking two of his ribs; despite the pain he gave orders to advance. Fearing that Wallace would fall back leaving the countryside desolated and deserted for the starving English, Edward was impatient to come to battle.

Uncharacteristically, Wallace decided to stand and fight. His disposition was as good as the terrain allowed, but it was a desperate gamble with inferior Scottish foot soldiers, supported by a small number of horsemen, confronted by ironclad cavalry and a well-trained force of longbowmen who could lay down a barrage of arrows to fall as thick as heavy rain, out-ranging the Scots' short bows.

Wallace deployed his infantry on a hill, now a district of Falkirk called Wallacestone. They formed four circles, or schiltroms, every man aiming a 12ft (4m) spear so that each schiltrom had the appearance of a giant porcupine. The front was defended by a stockade of long stakes driven into the ground and linked together with stout ropes. Wallace's cavalry, some 1,000 horses commanded by nobles, took up position at the rear. Between his position and the advancing English lay Westquarter Burn and a stretch of boggy ground. Somehow the English cavalry managed to cross the wet ground and, with their heavily armoured horses, soon knocked down the stockade to engage the schiltrom which held firm, many a rider being brought down on the end of a spear.

At the first charge of the English cavalry the Scottish cavalry fled the field, once again betraying Wallace at the last and critical moment. The Welsh bowmen now joined the battle and smothered the Scots with arrows. For a long time the schiltroms held, 'each stepping where his comrade stood the instant that he fell'. The Scottish defence was magnificent, justifying the discipline which Wallace had instilled in them. But eventually the schiltroms were breached. The slaughter which followed must have been horrific as the heavy English cavalry tore into them; a 12ft (4m) spear was an encumbrance rather than

ABOVE: *Sir John de Graeme's grave, Falkirk. He fought alongside Wallace from the time of Stirling Bridge until his death at the Battle of Falkirk.*

RIGHT: *The Wallace Monument at Wallacestone marks the site where the Scottish forces stood at the battle.*

a weapon in close combat. The death toll has been estimated at 10,000 to 15,000. Wallace fled to the safety of the woods to the north where the pursuing cavalry could not reach him.

ERECTED
to the
MEMORY
of that
CELEBRATED
SCOTTISH HERO
SIR WILLIAM
WALLACE
2nd AUGUST
1810

The Final Betrayal

The crushing defeat at Falkirk ended both Wallace's invincible reputation and his short rule. He held his last Scottish parliament at Torphichen where he resigned his position as Guardian of Scotland. It is not known if he was made to resign by the nobles who had never fully supported him, or if he went in disgust; but go he did, to spend the rest of his life as a guerilla fighter and outlaw. The two major and bitter rivals for the Scottish throne – Robert Bruce, Earl of Carrick, and John Comyn (the Red), nephew of John Balliol – became joint Guardians despite the fact that the latter had been in charge of the Scottish cavalry at Falkirk.

These nobles had no liking for the low-born Wallace, and once he was out of the way they put their rivalry aside and continued the war against Edward. On 20 January 1303 at Roslin near Edinburgh, with a force of about 8,000, they attacked and routed an English army. It was their last success. Edward returned and swept through Scotland, marking every step with blood and destruction. Oaths of fealty were once again given to him, and he granted a general amnesty to all those who fought for Scotland, allowing them to live in freedom and to retain their estates. Excluded from that amnesty was Wallace who was soon again declared an outlaw. There is some evidence that Wallace sailed to France to seek the support of the French king, Phillip IV, and the Pope. He and his knightly companions were given a financial allowance by Philip IV, and he is said to have been offered titles and an estate in France. His love for

ABOVE: The castle at Dumbarton. This is where Menteith led Wallace to believe he was being taken.

LEFT: Bruce Monument, Bannockburn. Bruce eventually succeeded Wallace and finally beat the English at the Battle of Bannockburn in 1314.

his country was too strong, however, and he returned to Scotland. From the autumn of 1299 to August 1305 history can tell us little of his activities, but it is certain that he and his companions continued to be a thorn in the side of the English.

Eventually he was betrayed by his friend and once fellow-patriot, Sir John de Menteith, to two of whose children he was godfather. By inducing a young nephew to become a member of Wallace's band, he became privy to the outlaw's movements. The nephew stole Wallace's arms while he slept and Menteith, to subdue him further, said that the house was surrounded by English soldiers, but if he came quietly he would be lodged comfortably in

Dumbarton as Edward had no wish to shed his blood. In the event, Wallace was taken through unpopulated parts of the country, for fear of his supporters, to Carlisle Castle where he was thrown into a dungeon. From there, under armed escort and roped to a horse, he endured a humiliating and painful 17-day journey to London.

The Death of Wallace

Wallace was led in a cavalcade into London but, because of the crowds blocking the streets leading to the Tower, he was lodged overnight in the house of a city alderman in Fenchurch Street. Next day he was taken, bound to a horse and accompanied by a large escort of knights, sheriffs, aldermen and the mayor, to the Great Hall at Westminster where he was seated on a bench and mocked with a crown of laurel. The king's justiciar, Sir Peter Mallory (Malorie), accused him of treason and various other crimes, to which Wallace replied that he could never have been a traitor to the King of England. Certainly Wallace had never acknowledged fealty to the English king, unlike so many so-called Scottish patriots. But Edward was not interested in legal niceties when it came to dealing with the one man who had always refused to submit to him and who, while he lived, would keep alive the flame of Scottish nationalism. It was inevitable that Wallace was immediately convicted.

ABOVE: Wallace crowned with laurel in Westminster Hall. Wallace was subjected to a mock coronation before suffering a barbaric death.

Afterwards, tied to the tails of two horses, he was dragged through the streets, pelted with stones and garbage, and brought to the common place of execution, the Elms in Smithfield near the present Barts Hospital. There he was barbarically

LEFT: Loudoun Hill, Irvine Valley, where Wallace avenged the death of his father by ambushing and killing Fenwick.

hanged, drawn and quartered, and one quarter each was sent for public exhibition in Newcastle, Berwick, Perth and Aberdeen in order to deter others. However much this treatment of a brave man might appal us, and be used as evidence of English brutality against the Scots, it was no more nor less than the mandatory punishment for traitors which had been introduced by the Normans in 1066, and which remained on the statute book until the end of the 18th century.

If Edward believed that the execution of Wallace was necessary in the national interest to bring about his peace between the two kingdoms, he was to be sadly mistaken. Within six months, Robert Bruce, Earl of Carrick – who had been pardoned by Edward and given possession of his family estates – took up arms against the king and, after murdering his rival John Comyn in 1306, had himself crowned at Scone. Edward invaded Scotland a third time and defeated Bruce, who promptly formed another army. Finally, in 1307 Edward, old and failing in health, set off on his fourth invasion of Scotland, but he died on the English side of the Solway Firth at Burgh-by-Sands.

William Wallace should be remembered not only for his great stature, superhuman strength and skill on the battlefield, but also for the compassionate and academic side to his character. Had circumstances been different he might well have risen to high estate in the Church. As a Marquess of Bute wrote: 'Sir William Wallace at least knew how to read and write three languages – namely his own and Latin and French, and it appears also that he knew Gaelic. He

RIGHT: Engraving of Wallace. Documents issued by Wallace from early 1298 add the Latin word miles *(knight) after his name.*

BELOW: Wallace statue, Edinburgh Castle.

knew the ancient and modern history, and the common simpler mathematics and science of his own day. … He had an unfading veneration for the Church … and a lifelong love for the Psalms which lasted until he died, with a priest holding the Psalter open, at his request, before his darkening eyes.' Blind Harry wrote of him:

IN TIME OF PEACE, MEEK AS A MAID WAS HE;
WHERE WAR APPROACHED, THE RIGHT
* HECTOR WAS HE.*
TO SCOTS MEN EVER CREDENCE GREAT HE
* GAVE;*
KNOWN ENEMIES COULD NEVER HIM
* DECEIVE.*

Scottish Nationhood

Edward I died in 1307 and Edward II, despite superior resources, was no match for the courage and military skill of Robert Bruce. Edward lost castle after castle until, in June 1314, Bruce put Edward to flight in the decisive Battle of Bannockburn, outside Stirling, and real independence was at last in Scotland's grasp. However, it was not until 1328, after Edward II had been deposed and murdered, that this independence was formally recognised by Edward III.

Not that the end of the Wars of Independence meant real peace between the two neighbours; border warfare flared up no less than 13 times between 1333 and 1547, often with the connivance or help of France, Scotland's partner in the 'auld alliance'.

A significant dynastic link was forged between Scotland and England in 1503 when James IV of Scotland married Margaret Tudor, daughter of Henry VII; though this did not prevent the death of James and the destruction of his army at Flodden, near Cold-stream, in 1513 at the hands of the forces of the young King Henry VIII. The defeat at Flodden led to Scotland's growing disillusionment with

*ABOVE: The **Stone of Destiny**, which was returned from Westminster to Scotland in November 1996. It is now kept, with the Honours of Scotland, in Edinburgh Castle.*

Bruce statue, Stirling Castle.